Discover

SOPHROLOGY

for your wellbeing

The study of human consciousness in harmony

LORENA LUCHIAN
Bucharest
2021

Discover

SOPHROLOGY

for your wellbeing

The study of human consciousness in harmony

ISBN 978-973-0-35348-8

I express my gratitude to my family
and my friends for always
being next to me.

Contents

Introduction

I first read about sophrology when studying psychology at university, in a class on *Creatology*, given by Dr. Anca Munteanu, the author of the book *Insights of Creatology*, a comprehensive and fascinating volume dealing with the multi-dimensional range of this subject. In the book, several approaches to improving creativity, different types of psychotherapies, brainstorming and different types of relaxation such as the Silva method, hypnotherapy, sophrology and other approaches were examined. All these methods are designed to facilitate our access to our inner world.

Relaxation, symbiosis between the psychic and the somatic, sophrology, inducing calmness, visualization, unconsciousness, creativity and alpha waves, were all ideas which made me think of the resources we have and the ways we can use them in order to make our life more beautiful.

Quoting the above mentioned book, "Starting with the etymological, the term *sophrology* signifies the science of harmonizing consciousness. Promoting a holistic vision of the human being (which extends a well-established ancient Chinese tradition), it seeks to establish a new balance between our three elements: body, mind, and spirit. This new conception triggers another way of seeing, and to a healthy life, causing changes which extend into the medical field."

Wishing to deepen my knowledge and understanding of this science of *the spirit in harmony*, both for personal interest and for its possible therapeutic application in my work as a psychotherapist, I attended a sophrology school in Geneva, Switzerland, and I became a sophrologist.

Through sophrology, I entered a fascinating universe of the body, mind, and spirit. Practicing the exercises, helped me to become more aware of my emotions, my thoughts, and the way that they merge with my body. I felt positive "without any reason", I started to see the world more objectively and to take the people as they are. I gained greater mental clarity and internal power. I learned to listen with all my body, and to appreciate the messages I received from inside and from outside. I didn't visualize, I didn't project things, I didn't imagine a situation happening but instead, I came to be present in my body and to go deeper into the depth of my being. I became one with my body.

This intimate connection with the body filled me with quietness and peace. Any one of us can be transformed when we start to take responsibility for our beliefs, emotions, actions, and behavior.

I invite you to start this journey into yourself. You will rediscover yourself, you will set in motion your vital force, your capacities, and you will attain a serene consciousness, a relaxed body and a clear, alert mind.

The sophrology training consists of simple and efficient exercises that lead to a more positive outlook, greater concentration and focus, a more relaxed approach to life, greater optimism, and you will be able to deal more easily with life's challenges. Regular practice puts you in touch with your body and with all the sensations and messages that are revealed by it. A conscious reconnection with your body brings you closer to the present moment, quiets your mind, makes you more calm, and all these have a favorable effect of your health at all levels, positively transforming your whole life.

This book consists of three chapters. The first chapter describes simple but important ideas regarding the connection between the body, mind, and emotions, together with short exercises you can do while you are reading. In the second chapter, I described the theories, the concepts and the terminology of sophrology, as they were elaborated by the founder of sophrology, Dr. Alfonso Caycedo. In the third chapter, you will become more familiar with the development of the exercises.

Before you start, please find a little journal where you can write, after each exercise, whatever you noticed and observed during the practice, that is to describe the sensations and perceptions offered by the body.

CHAPTER ONE

Becoming aware of our body,
our emotions and our mind

Our body seeks our attention

What if we were to start giving more attention to the body that we are living in? Not just at the superficial level, but at a deep, profound level. How would it be? I hope you will find the answer in this book, through the practice of sophrology.

The relationship we have with our body tells a lot about us, because there is a strong connection between the body, the emotions and the mind, or, to put it better, they influence each other continuously. Your negative feelings, frustrations, agitation and stress, always have an echo in the body, generating muscular tensions, varying in depth and intensity, depending on the triggers. In the body, we find the effects of all our thoughts and emotions, which sometimes turn into symptoms, and sometimes remain there, dormant, indicating discomfort. The body is always the place where these are manifested, but we are unaware of them because we do not know our body – which is the expression of our inner world. Through it joy, sadness, passions, cheerfulness, crying and tensions surface. The body takes the form of the emotions that it experiences.

To know our body, we have to listen to it. The body constantly transmits messages, some more subtle, some more powerful. Our body wants to be heard, to be given attention. But we don't really pay attention to our body unless it gives us strong sensations such as hunger, sexual desire, pain; "I have a headache", "I'm sick", "My stomach hurts", "Ouch, I hit myself". But why don't we use positive expressions to describe the pleasant sensations of our bodies? Why don't we learn to know it, to appreciate it, to savor it?

Instead of having a body, we can *be* our body, we can fuse with its feelings, its sensations, and we can reconnect with ourselves. Our body is a whole universe full of life. When we direct our attention inwards, we are connecting with our own wisdom. We have got used to living with a mind-body dissociation – the mind is in one place, and the body is here, now. It would be something new for us to "reunify" them by connecting with the depths of our being.

The body knows how to develop a life, another human universe, from two separate cells that come together in an act of creation. The cells are the smallest forms of life, tiny units which build the entire organism, and can perform all the activities necessary for survival, providing basic functions: nutrition, reproduction, movement. Likewise, the cells of the body are "trained" so that when they become mature they are specialized to be blood cells, muscle cells, nerve cells, or another type of cells. Cells' forms depend on the roles they fulfill in the body. A group of similar cells come together to form tissues, organs, and the whole organism. Inside each cell numerous processes take place which ensure its survival, further ensuring the good functioning of the whole body, that is of the person.

There are inside us, "intelligent" life forms that know what to do for us to function normally and be healthy. The cells know how to remedy, repair and eliminate toxins ensuring homeostasis, the internal balance of the body.

In a way, we can say that the cell is a complex being who is born, feeds, moves, specializes in a field, communicates, reproduces itself and dies. Like a human being, if we make a simple comparison. We are born, we move, we specialize in one domain, we communicate, and we die. There is a similarity that makes me think of the question "whose cells are we?" Perhaps we are the cells of a higher organism for which we have to ensure homeostasis. Maybe this organism is planet Earth, or maybe that we are the cells of a larger system... known or unknown to us.

But until we manage to find the answers to this *radical* question, the aim of sophrology is to reconnect with our body and with its infinite intelligence. Sensory function is the first thing that sophrology tries to reactivate. This function is not incompatible with reasoning, on the contrary, there could be no reasoning without sensoriality. The brain needs sensory stimulation to exist.

Through the exercises we will be able to understand the potential of our *corporality*, the energy that we possess and the positive aspects that are already integrated at the physical level. The body is the source of our vitality, motivation, inspiration and, most importantly, it is our inner guidance, it knows better than the mind what is best for us. It knows what it likes and it feels good when we are happy. Energy and vitality are internal manifestations generated by physical, mental, and emotional stimuli.

Sophrological exercises don't require complicated postures and movements, nor special attire. These help us to turn our attention towards the inside, and the fusion between mind and body will mobilize our physical energy and will boost our awareness.

We can start becoming conscious of the organic balances and imbalances, be gentler with our body, show love, acceptance, and care to it. Everything we have to know is already inside us, so why don't we take it into consideration, feeling and trusting in the silent or less silent language of our body? Whoever does not affirm the body, doesn't have a body. The awareness of our presence underlies an extraordinary strengthening of confidence. You can demonstrate this to yourself through the practice of sophrology.

I invite you now to do an exercise, noticing how the mind activates the sensations when it is directed to a specific part of the body:

Become fully aware of your hands, and notice the physical sensations
in the skin, fingers, nails, palm, back of your hands...

Focus your entire attention and stay concentrated on them for a minute or two, observing
with curiosity and wonder all the physical sensations...

Switch your attention only
onto the right hand,
observing the sensations that appear in the skin, palm, fingers, nails, back of the hand...
And stay concentrated on your right hand for a while...

Now compare them.
How does the right one feel,
how does the left one feel?
Is there any difference?
What is it?

The relation body-mind-emotions

When we consciously use all our senses at the same time, there appears a feeling of union and merging with all the internal sensations that the body reveals. It is the feeling of presence and stillness. We hear, see, smell, touch, taste, all at the same time. Our consciousness is in the body, now, in the present moment. We are calm, alert and lucid. We become simply observers, and the mind doesn't have time for unnecessary "comments", it is not busy judging and ruminating on the information, or creating "stories". We are ourselves, we are not identified with the mind.

The physical body is solid and is always in the present. It has shape, we can feel it and touch it. The mind instead, can be anywhere, it is fluid and it's "flying" in the past or in the future, bringing in the body different emotions. And each one of us knows how far and in which directions our thoughts turn. The stories created by the mind are often appalling. We have anxious thoughts about the future and regretful thoughts about the past. If we think of the past, we interpret and reinterpret events that anyway cannot be changed. If we think about the future, we are worried about something that might happen, or waiting for a certain moment that will give us joy. But we are rarely fully present. Through the body, we can be again present, be here and now, with the body.

Due to its ceaseless activity, the mind pulls us away from what we are, it disconnects us from our being. A scattered mind imbalances us emotionally.

"Mind, in the way I use this word, is not just thought. It includes your emotions as well as all unconscious mental-emotional reactive patterns. Emotion arises at the place where mind and body meet. It is the body's reaction to your mind – or you might say, a reflection of your mind in the body. For example, an attack thought or a hostile thought will create a build-up of energy in the body that we call anger. The body is getting ready to fight. The thought that you are being threatened, physically or psychologically, causes the body to contract, and this is the physical side of what we call fear. Research has shown that strong emotions even cause changes in the biochemistry of the body. These biochemical changes represent the physical or material aspect of emotion. Of course, you are not usually conscious of all your thought patterns, and it is often only through watching your emotions that you can bring them into awareness." Eckhart Tolle – *The power of now.*

The notion of *observing* thoughts occurs not only in oriental traditions or in spiritual literature, it is one of the main methods of psychological research. "The method of observation is the most frequently used, and from the technical point of view, it's the easiest to apply because it doesn't require sophisticated equipment, often a pencil and a notebook is enough. It is also the first method, from a historical perspective, that people used for understanding and describing the moods and behaviors of others." Mihai Golu – *The Fundamentals of General Psychology.*

Since observation of external phenomena represents one of the main instruments of psychological knowledge, we can observe *ourselves* to know ourselves better and bring to light the contents of our being. Self-observation brings about deep changes in neuronal activity; when we are not aware of ourselves, most of our thoughts are impulsive.

Thoughts are like "children" of the mind, and are mostly uncontrolled, useless, repetitive, negative, and don't come true. We "develop" these untrue thoughts endlessly. In addition, we have the tendency to emphasize the negative side of things, as if negative and hostile thoughts are more seductive. We can analyze what someone did or did not do, said or did not say, reviving and repeating mentally the same ideas, and all these thought patterns are absorbing our entire attention.

Every thought we have creates a cascade of biochemical changes in the body, and each cell communicates instantly with the others. Our mental activity influences the internal balance of the body. Our body is connected with emotions and with our mental life. It cries with pain, vibrates with joy and enthusiasm, and strains with tension. For example, if we watch an exciting or dramatic movie, our body releases stress hormones, the heart begins to beat faster – the body reacts as if the action is real. If the movie is positive, if we watch a comedy or a beautiful story, the body reacts by releasing other types of substances, which give us positive feelings and creates a good mood due to our mental activity and associated emotions. Beautiful dreams make us feel good at the physical and emotional level, but we all know very well the psychosomatic effects of nightmares. So, as we can see, our thoughts influence our bodies, and their effect varies according to their intensity.

Just because our heads are filled with thoughts and judgments, this doesn't mean that we are mindful of what we are doing. Thoughts are crushing and flocking into the mind, seizing our attention. They are "consuming". It is tiring to live only through the mind, forgetting our body. Conversely, if we fill the body with our attention, the mind settles down and it becomes clear. Even when we are in the middle of intense intellectual activity, the thinking must be focused, "united" for better results. By keeping a part of attention in the body, during any activity, we improve both the quality of the work and the quality of our physical and emotional state due to the feeling of presence and serenity that comes from the union of the mind with the body.

Through awareness of our thoughts and beliefs, we have the power to change the things we do not like in ourselves, and we became more balanced, permitting in this way the emergence of a personality with new dimensions. Becoming observers of our thoughts, we create a space (*Phronic Region*)[1] where we do not identify with thinking. This new space activates consciousness, the base of human existence.

The following exercise enables you to notice the difference between being absorbed by thinking and becoming aware of the sensations of your body:

Sit comfortably, close your eyes and
let yourself drown in the flow of thoughts. Follow them.
They "run" from one notion to another, multiplying
endless ideas.

Notice what you feel and where...
And now, bring your attention inwards, become
aware of your body,
your breath, and your physical sensations.
Fill in the body with your entire attention.

Be here, now, for a few minutes,
leaving all the thoughts to one side.

---

[1] Term introduced by Prof. Caycedo to designate an interior space created during the practice of sophrology exercises. More about the Phronic Region to page 68.

*Even if they appear, keep your attention on the body, from the top of the head
to the tip of the toes...*
Observe how you feel now and stay a little bit more connected to your body.

Indeed, western education favors thinking, neglecting, even denying the importance of the body. But thinking cannot control the emotions, which are profound and powerful compulsions that cannot be blocked by any reasoning. An increase in emotion enhances the muscular tensions, which, in turn, will boost the growth of emotions. This is the game between body, emotions, and thoughts. Sometimes it is pleasant and exuberant, and sometimes it is confusing and threatening.

Some people suffered a lot and decided to inhibit any kind of emotion. They remain "cold" in the face of events, whatever these may be. They don't allow themselves to feel. Emotions don't come to the surface, creating an effect of suppressing – and at some point they will come out powerfully. Others keep their emotions hidden behind sophisticated masks, and when we penetrate beyond these masks, we discover a real emotional coloring that we didn't previously have access to.

Sophrological training helps us become aware of emotions and notice how they feel in our body so that we can more easily process, manage, and control their manifestations. Emotions play an important role in balance. We have to be friends with our emotions, to enjoy the positive and accept and neutralize the negative.

If we want to feel good and positively influence the biochemistry of the body, we have to become aware of our mental atmosphere and focus our attention on the things, events, and thoughts that make us feel good and that give us pleasure, like agreeable images, emotions, feelings, and memories. Events and emotions are stored together in the memory. When we have a pleasant disposition, we store positive things, when we are in an unhappy state, we store negative things. We tend to pay attention to the information corresponding to our state of mind.

One of the principles of sophrology is that of mobilizing our resources through positive thoughts and actions. Life and people, in general, give us enough negativity. Whoever wants to see negative things will see only those. Whoever wants to see the positive, will concentrate on those. We can encourage the positive in us to flourish and cultivate joy, moment by moment because we know this is a much healthier way of living. Bringing our attention to the body, to the physical sensations offered by it, facilitates this

process and, as a result, we create that interior space
that has the gift of leading us to a state of calm.

Tension-Relief

As we have already seen, our body is the "house"
of the accumulated emotions. Fear can manifest itself
as tension in the neck, back, and jaw. Anger in fists
clenched, rippled forehead, wrinkled lips. Joy in the
heart and abdomen. A human face can "speak" without
saying a word, just by a look. Body posture is an
indication of the state of the spirit, a person can be
tensed, crouched, rigid, open and relaxed, or at ease.

Therapists know that the people are bent by
the weight of the emotional luggage they carry.
Accumulated tensions remain for a long time stored in
the muscles and tissues of the body, becoming "the
natural state" and only after we do a tension-release
exercise do we realize the strain we felt before. When
we give our body the attention that it deserves, we put
in motion its healing positive energy, mobilizing and
activating its resources.

Through simple exercises for tension-relief, we
provoke contractions in order to be able to perceive
the sensations generated by these tensions. In this
way, we can make a distinction between tension and
relaxation, and we can better observe the contrasts of

the physical tensions, choosing to experience the pleasant sensations of our corporality.

Unprocessed psychological pain (which is repressed or not fully lived) remains in the body, and we express it, often without being aware of it, through physical illnesses. All unexpressed negative feelings can take the form of somatic and psychosomatic disorders. Buried psychological and emotional tensions are often revealed by tensions. Therefore it is better to express our anger, suffering, and sadness in a healthy way, and there are plenty of effective ways for this: talking to a psychotherapist, freeing ourselves through writing, doing exercise, watching a comedy, hitting a pillow or talking to a friend. It is more beneficial to acknowledge and work with these painful feelings than to attack others with our poison or to poison ourselves by repressing feelings, engaging in self-blame, lack of self-esteem and respect, or engaging in different kinds of addictions, including food addiction.

So, let's manifest more self-love, care, and attention, starting with the body we live in. The body doesn't lie, so it is better to work in a deep and conscious symbiosis with it, listen to its messages, and consider it our friend.

Notice how your body feels before, during, and after the following exercise:

Close your eyes and relax
as much as possible.
Tighten your fist and arm, contracting
the muscles of your arm,
but the rest of the body remains relaxed.
Do not tighten your jaw at the same time...
Observe how the tension is accumulating, and
notice the sensations as they occur...

Now release and relax all the tensions from your
arm and hand, while loosening your entire body a little bit
more...
With closed eyes, receive the sensations
that arrive.
Give a name to these perceptions
(heat, tingling, sensation of heaviness, lightness).

Compare what you feel in the activated arm with
the sensations from the other arm.

Do you feel the same?
Repeat the exercise twice more with
short pauses between them.
Then repeat the exercise, activating the other arm.

This exercise is very relaxing, especially when
we tense and release the whole body, a part at a time.

After a few minutes of practice, the body becomes lighter and more relaxed. Muscular release after tension allows a deepening, a profound relaxation of the whole body, and also a mental relaxation, which improves concentration.

Acquiring a method of stress relief and physical and mental relaxation is a gift we give to ourselves because we want to be happy and enjoy the psychological state of wellbeing. It's true that we also have to face different and various unpleasant experiences that are part of life. But our goal is not to let ourselves be overwhelmed by them in the long term, and to do what we can in order to get out from the morass of negativity.

Stress and Relaxation

When people describe stress they say, "I'm confused, nervous, and frustrated!", "My heart is beating fast and my blood pressure has increased", in other words, they mention changes related to the way they feel and think. Physical reactions to stress are usual accompanied by emotional responses. If the stress is maintained over a long period of time, it becomes chronic and can seriously affect our physical, psychological, and emotional health.

Faced with the many forms of stress in daily life, we try to find different rational explanations for what is happening. But when our reasons are not enough to explain our unpleasant states – anguish, deprivation, misery, misfortune, we take refuge in illness, a way of being temporarily or permanently sheltered from the responsibility of assuming our lives. This is an innate survival response, a defense mechanism. Running away seems to be the best solution in the face of a danger we cannot overcome. However, running away is not the best solution, especially when "threats" are more and more numerous and varied.

Stress is an adaptation mechanism people feel as a result of adverse, difficult situations. Stressors are environmental events or conditions, sufficiently intense or frequent that produce physiological, psychological, and social reactions in the person. A lot of research has been already done, and many books were written about stress and its impact on the body. On a physical level, chronic stress can manifest itself by lowering the immune system, causing muscle tension, heart disease, shallow breathing, blood pressure problems, insomnia, and sexual problems. At the emotional level, it can take the form of anger, irritability, nervousness, anxiety, hostility, depression, or restlessness. At the cognitive level, it can manifest itself in the deterioration of the memory, increasingly making mistakes and getting things wrong, indecision, reduced concentration, and negativity. All these lead to problematic behaviors such as addiction, drug use, eating disorders, family problems, and so on.

The sources of stress factors come both from external circumstances (the atmosphere in the workplace, the lack of a job, profession, family, school, environment, contemporary society) and internal (temperament, criticism, self-control, way of thinking, approach to problems solving). More generally, the world in which we live is characterized by stress and an over-loading with information that permanently distracts our attention (beeps, WhatsApp, Viber, Facebook, Instagram, the internet, thousands of articles and headlines mostly negative, ringing phones, people who talk non-stop), so we have to use all our resources, capacities, and forces if we want our life to be marked by a PLUS and not by a MINUS.

In our most stressful moments, we feel as though we are being pulled in millions of different directions, physically, emotionally, psychologically, mentally, and spiritually. A "disintegration" of our being takes place and we don't always manage to recover completely after it, because we do not give ourselves time and attention. There are always "more important" things to do. And all this influence the other aspects of our life: health, our reactions towards others, and our relationship with our partner, family, friends, and colleagues.

Everyone should identify their personal stress factors and should become aware of their reactions to stress. Most of the time, these behaviors are not good for us, nor for others. And it happens often, perhaps daily or several times a day, that things are not as we want or expect them to be. Every day we are confronted with bigger or smaller disappointments, but we cannot allow agitation, discontent, and disappointment to take control of our lives.

Dr. Wayne Dyer describes stress as something that is only in our minds, he says that stress doesn't exist; there are only people who emanate stressful thoughts. That means we have to change our vision, to live joyfully and not fearfully, to feel happy that we are alive. We can deliberately choose to flip the switch from the pressure we put upon ourselves so that we live more peacefully and are more aware - a rearrangement of our lives to minimize the impact of the stressors.

If stress is a state of mind that can be changed, we just have to decide to approach life more playfully, to have a positive attitude towards it, to cultivate a healthy lifestyle, and to do something different every day. Everybody knows this, but how many of us really put these ideas into practice? We forget to breath consciously, eat healthy, move our bodies, enjoy, and practice relaxation techniques. Some hide behind the excuse "I don't have time". In fact, do we really have no time to live, to enjoy life, and do the things that are good for us? But it seems we always have time to worry, stress, sit on a couch and watch TV instead of doing good, pleasant and constructive things that could give quality to our life.

Let's look at how the exercises in this book enable you to reconnect with your inner soul, which doesn't know anything about stress. And if you try not to believe everything your mind tells you, you will find that life can be more enjoyable and that stress will be alleviated.

A simple exercise I recommend is:

Watch carefully what happens with your breath when you are nervous;

Become aware of your breathing in stressful moments;

Notice how a person breathes when tensed or agitated.

Breath

The following exercise it is an example of conscious breathing. Please try it before you go on reading.

Become aware of your breathing.

*Focus your attention on your breath
and listen to your body...*

Do you breathe? Yes, but how do you breathe?
*Is your breath slow, soothing, deep, and
abdominal?*
*Or it is rather shallow, uneven, and incomplete?
How do you feel?*

*Now, please close your eyes, and
for a few minutes, breathe in and breathe out calmly,
slowly, noticing how your stomach moves
in and out while you are inhaling
and exhaling...*
*Notice the physical
sensations associated with breathing and keep
your attention on the body...*

*Breathe... Contemplate yourself...
Seek the presence... Fill your whole body with your
attention...*

It seems that something has changed. The mind is quieter, and a subtle feeling of wellbeing arises.

And if only a few minutes of relaxation, by becoming aware of our body and breath helps us calm down and refresh our consciousness, why not do it every day? Proper breathing adds quality to our life, makes us feel good and energetic, and can cure some illnesses.

The first thing we do when we come into this world is *inhale,* and the last thing we do when we leave this world is *exhale.* Breathing represents a special connection between mind and body, between the *immaterial* and the *material.* Breath unites these two moments, and keeping our attention on them reminds us that we are *one.*

Here are some ideas about breathing and its benefits.

Diaphragmatic (abdominal) breathing is the correct way to breathe, where the stomach is going in and out as we inhale and exhale. People think they breathe correctly, but actually, they just take in a "sufficient" amount of oxygen to live. And this is neither the best nor the healthiest way to breathe. Diaphragmatic breathing has a calming effect on both the body and the mind, decreases anxiety, and oxygenates the body. When we breathe correctly, we cannot be stressed or if we are, the stress diminishes significantly because the air penetrates deep into the body, calms down the nervous system, and gives a "massage" to the internal organs.

Abdominal breathing stimulates the vagus nerve, and this nerve releases a substance that counteracts the effects of stress hormones. That's why we use breathing in various anxiety disorders as a therapeutic technique. And we can say it has a result like that of a tranquilizer but a natural tranquilizer, produced by our own body.

Abdominal breathing is natural, and it happens by itself if we relax. During sleep, when the body loosens up, our breathing is not superficial anymore. We don't breathe in the chest but from the stomach because breathing takes its natural course. Children always breathe properly, and we can see how their stomach inflates and deflates while breathing.

Conscious abdominal breathing releases the tensions accumulated by the body. When we are stressed, upset, or angry, our entire body is bent, breathing becomes shallow, and the body doesn't get the oxygen it needs.

Breathing is one of the most important ways for the body to detoxify itself, so we should help it and work with it in order to achieve and maintain balance. Perhaps not coincidentally the lungs are the only internal organs that we can control consciously. Even with a few deep breaths that we do every morning, we help the entire body to be oxygenated and ready for the day. In this way, our cells will receive vital information, will understand that we have chosen life and that we want to live.

*For example, you can breathe
 out until the air goes totally out from your lungs,
then breathe in deeply to the tips of the toes...*

Respiration releases emotional tensions, "washing" the emotional currents that sometimes seem to be coming from all sides. The body unconsciously shows this through sighs, suspiration, or long deep breaths. The breathing exercises also release the negative emotions trapped in the chest and abdomen.

Breathing improves body posture. If we are aware and breathe properly, our body posture automatically changes.

Breathing helps internal processes, including cellular regeneration, thanks to efficient oxygenation.

Conscious breathing settles us down and refreshes our body and mind. Many of us simply do not know that we do not breathe properly. But we can start experimenting and see how we feel and how our body reacts if we give ourselves a few minutes of deep breaths every day. In the morning, on an empty stomach, is a good time of the day to practice breathing exercises because we need our body to be oxygenated and energized throughout the day. It is like making a pact with our body, saying "I love you, I take care of you, so every day I give you a few minutes to fill you up with the oxygen you need so much".

Honoring this daily program, where you stay only with yourself, is an important step in keeping stress out of your life.

Intuition

Sophrology utilizes three types of energy: physical energy – the body, what we see, feel, touch, hear, and smell, vital energy – our life force, the energy that keeps us alive and that is animated by breathing, fueled by food and controlled by thought, and spiritual energy – the things we know without knowing how we know them, coincidences in life, brilliant ideas that we have, the solutions that come from "nowhere". Everyone can say they have experienced moments that cannot be logically explained. This means that everybody has intuition, especially women, but it is stifled by rationality, which always puts doubt ahead of intuition, always searching for evidence.

Intuition manifests itself, like emotions, at the body level. Sometimes in the form of images, or as an impulse, or as a kind of "knowing", and sometimes as an interior monologue that we can listen to or not. Its language seems difficult to understand because it is a symbolic language whose messages reason doubts. It is something that occurs beyond reason, it is the feeling that we know something without being able to explain how and why, a direct penetration into the essence of a problem, a revelation. Intuition develops and manifests itself when reason is less active, when we are detached and relaxed. When we are more advanced along the path of sophrological training, we have moments where we connect deeply with this deep center of our being which sometimes "suggests" things, gives us beautiful and amazing ideas that we have not thought of, and makes us act in a new and different way, with the certainty that is good for us.

CHAPTER TWO

The theories and concepts of sophrology

A short history

Sophrology was created in 1960 by Doctor Alfonso Caycedo, a neuropsychiatrist, in Madrid. Even though at that time there were already various relaxation techniques and associated therapeutic concepts, Dr. Caycedo's medical practice, his research, and his studies, made him increasingly interested in human consciousness and psychosomatic medicine. At that time there was the word *schizophrenia,* which meant a *split in consciousness* but there was no word or way of describing consciousness when it was in harmony. In this way, sophrology was born.

Caycedo's goal was to create a form of therapy that took account of the idea that disease unbalances the body, both the mind, and the spirit and that both of these should be addressed simultaneously. With his method of therapy he didn't just want to cure diseases, but also to help people to know themselves better and live in harmony with themselves. Sophrology helps us to become aware of our bodies and our minds. It is about rebalancing on a holistic level, by harmonizing the body, the mind and the spirit.

The etymology of the word comes from the Greek language: *sos = harmony, equilibrium, phren = consciousness, spirit and logos = study, science.*

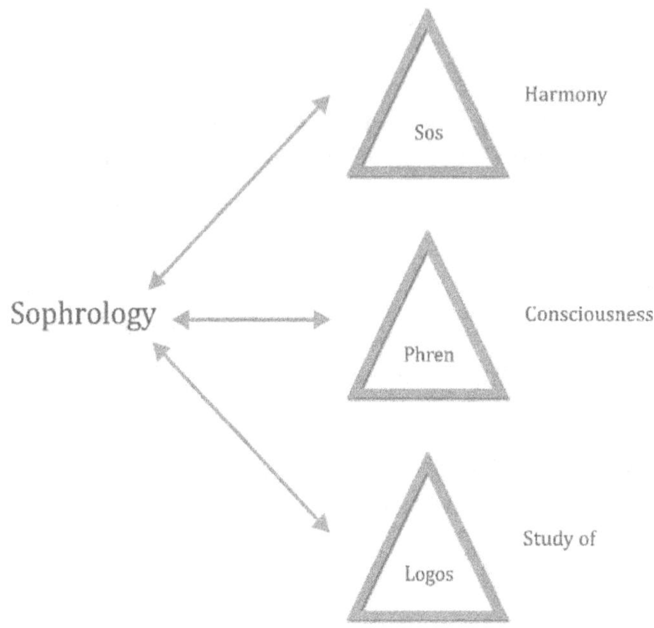

Sophrology is the study of human consciousness in harmony, and it is based on a series of dynamic relaxation exercises that are focused on the corporal perception and the relation between body, mind, and spirit. These physical and mental exercises are easy to do, can be done anytime, anywhere, and if they are practiced regularly, they can help us to attain a relaxed body and a calm, agile mind.

The first things people start to notice when they practice sophrology are more restful sleep, better concentration, fewer worries, increased self-confidence, and a sense of inner happiness. So, by practicing sophrology, we can develop a state of clear, uncluttered consciousness and a state of inner harmony and wellbeing. The aim of these static and dynamic exercises is to conquer and consolidate the balance between mind, emotions, and body, stimulating positive qualities and resources that we have to improve health, quality of life, and personal fulfillment. The exercises include breathing techniques, simple body movements and mental activation strategies for self-knowledge and the expansion of consciousness, and also relaxation and approaches to using one's imagination as a means of developing psychophysical harmony. Regular practice leads to a positive transformation in our attitude towards ourselves and the world around us.

Alfonso Caycedo was born on 19th November 1932 in Bogota, Colombia, where he lived the early part of his life. Once he had completed his general education, he moved to Madrid to study medicine at a Spanish university. He specialized in psychiatry and neurology under the direction of Ibor Lopez, a professor of psychiatry. During his medical practice at the hospital in Madrid, Caycedo became interested in both ancient and modern methods of altering states

of consciousness. He felt that medicine studied
everything except consciousness.

Alfonso Caycedo created sophrology in order to
to provide a method for investigating human consciousness and he set up a department of
psychosomatic medicine and clinical sophrology in the
University of Madrid. The method was designed to
help patients get better quickly, using as little
medication and psychiatric treatment as possible.

In 1961, at the 5th International Congress of
Psychotherapy, Caycedo presented the term of
sophrology, to the academic world.

Ibor Lopez suggested to Caycedo that he go to Switzerland to work with the renowned Swiss psychiatrist, Ludwig Binswanger, a friend of his, known for the influence he had on the development of phenomenological and existential psychology.

At the Bellevue clinic in Switzerland (Kreutzlingen), the approach was very different, they had another way of seeing their patients compared with the rest of Europe, where some physically damaging classical psychiatry treatments (such as electroshocks) prevailed. In Kreutzlingen, the focus was on the human contact between doctor and patient, and on the *presence* of the doctor and the attention given to the patient. Under the guidance of "the master Binswanger" as Dr. Caycedo called him, he became interested in phenomenology.

Phenomenology became the base of sophrology, as a method for investigating consciousness.[2] Caycedo did not deepen his study of consciousness just by

---

[2] Phenomenology — from the Greek language *phainomenon* and *logos*, the study of phenomena. It is an idealistic movement founded by Husserl which proposes the interpretation of phenomena of consciousness through „intentionality" (orientation towards something) and meaning (content), putting in parenthesis the external reality. In Hegel's view, *Phenomenology of Spirit* describes the successive phases of the spirit in its evolution from „sensory certainty" to „absolute knowing". Phenomena – an outward manifestation of the essence of a thing; something that in some way manifests; what is given or directly perceived.

working with the patients from the hospital, where he had access to patients with a *pathological consciousness*. In Madrid, Caycedo had already used clinical hypnosis, because, he said, when we talk about consciousness, we have to study all the procedures that in one form or another can influence it, and hypnosis was a technique that he had available to him. At that time, people claimed that sophrology was merely hypnosis under a different name. Hypnosis was already being studied in the medical world, and electroencephalograms showed the changes that took place in consciousness during hypnotherapeutical practice. But at the same time, he also noticed that many patients were cautious when it came to hypnosis, a term which had become associated with something mysterious or magical.

Besides hypnosis, there were other methods of relaxation and other ways of altering consciousness, as Schultz autogenic training method, Jacobson's relaxation technique, and others.

In Switzerland, Caycedo met Dr. Abrezol, a dentist, who became the ambassador for sophrology. He began to use it both on himself and in his work with his patients. As a result of his sophrology practice, he began to have outstanding results when he played tennis, so he began using the method to improve the performance of athletes; he started by helping a friend with whom he played tennis regularly, and his performance and concentration increased dramatically. Then he helped another friend to improve their skiing performance. Due to these excellent results, he ventured into the world of sport. Using this form of mental training, he gave Swiss skiers a vitality and an élan which enabled them to collect an incredible number of medals in the '60s and '70s.

Abrezol never ceased to develop, learn and teach sophrology. "Regular practice of sophrology allowed me to discover, conquer and transform my own consciousness." Dr. Raymond Abrezol – *La Sophrologie Ici et Maintenant.*

In order to deepen his study of human consciousness, between 1964 and 1966, Caycedo travelled to India, Tibet, and Japan, because "Easterners understand consciousness better than us, western psychiatrists". They have studied pure consciousness for thousands of years. "Go talk to them, live with them", his teacher told him.

Although he was newly married and had a career as a doctor in front of him, Caycedo decided to go to India. The six months he planned for this trip turned into two years. There, he discovered a new world. "In the same way that some people collect coins, I collected ideas about consciousness", Caycedo said. And India was filled with such ideas. During his stay in the East, he published a book, *Letters of Silence,* a dialogue with all types of yoga masters. He made contact with, and entered into discussions with Indian doctors, both psychiatrists and those who were using yoga as therapy.

There are many types of yoga. These various methods aim at "conquering" the body, and in that they encompass all the bodily, physiological, and psychological functions. Through the body, we can make the transition from an everyday consciousness to a higher consciousness, also called hyperconsciousness. Indians believe that accessing this type of consciousness is a path that brings them into contact with the divine, and the key to this process is *contemplation*. This is not passive contemplation, daydreaming but contemplation by one who seeks *the presence*.

Western theories were speculative instead; there were books containing philosophical texts trying to explain consciousness, but no technique was described. The body did not exist. Nor was the body mentioned in psychoanalysis.

We can describe sophrology as a synthesis of traditional eastern healing techniques and therapies (Taoism, Yoga, Tibetan medicine, and Zen) and western influences (Phenomenology).

Following his studies into to human consciousness and inspired by oriental techniques and disciplines, in 1967, at the Clinical Hospital in Barcelona, Caycedo devised Sophro-Dynamic Relaxation (SDR), a coherent and structured method that includes specific exercises adapted to a western lifestyle. Sophrology was not trying to transpose eastern methods but adapt the content of these processes, with great respect for the disciplines.

He proposed the term "Dynamic Relaxation" to describe the method used in sophrology. The goal was to practice it for therapeutic and preventive purposes.

Over the years, sophrology has been presented at numerous international medical congresses. Sophrology has developed and expanded into several countries in Europe, being very popular in Belgium, Italy, and Switzerland. In France, it is extremely fond of, there are many schools, practices, and books about sophrology. Though sophrology originates in the medical sphere, today it is particularly prevalent in French and Spanish speaking countries, as a way of relaxation and self-knowledge, with applications in different fields.

Natalia Caycedo, the daughter of Alfonso Caycedo, a doctor who specialized in psychiatry, neurophysiology, and neuropsychology, continues his work at the International Institute of Caycedian Sophrology in Barcelona.

In 1989, Dorna Revie began studying sophrology with Pascal Mottet, translated the course into English, and in 1990 started running classes in English. In this way, sophrology became available also to the English speakers, through the school Dorna runs in Geneva[3]. In 2000, Revie completed a master Sophrology Diploma with Caycedo and in 2003 completed the Trainer Training Program that permits her to train sophrologists.

Caycedo deceased in September 2017. He has dedicated his entire life to the unceasing investigation of consciousness, to the promotion of the values of the human being and, in many different parts of the world, to the formation of thousands of people in his beautiful work – sophrology.[4]

Professor Caycedo will always be remembered for his strength, his enthusiasm, his great intuition, his intelligence, and above all, his love for his family and his profession.

Sophro-Dynamic Relaxation (SDR)

Sophro-Dynamic Relaxation comprises three cycles. The first cycle has four levels and is called

---

[3] Energy Centre Sàrl, www.energycentre.ch

[4] For more information on the history of sophrology, study the first three links presented at Resources. In the video on YouTube, you can watch Dr. Caycedo talking about sophrology, this being also the source of some quotations in this chapter.

"Fundamental", the second cycle is called "Radical", and the third, "Existential".

The 1ˢᵗ cycle – Fundamental

LEVEL ONE (SDR 1) is inspired by yoga. By practicing the exercises at this level, we become more aware of the body in which we live, the form, the shape, and physical sensations. We learn to breathe deeply and to gradually eliminate the physical tensions which we have accumulated.

At this level, we are encouraged to notice in our body the effects of the pleasant experiences, the positive somatic sensations, especially at the level of the skin, and the feeling of being happy to be alive. These are generated by moments when we feel good, by small and enjoyable things like a beautiful smile, an agreeable emotion, a favorite melody, a nice gesture, a special event, or daily moments of joy; the emphasis is on the experience of these events in our body and on the physical sensations that appear.

We learn to live in the present, without judgment, to see the world "as if for the first time", and to become intimately aware of the physical structures and functions of our body. The body scheme and the representation we have for our body are fundamental to sophrology exercises.

LEVEL TWO (SDR 2) is inspired by Buddhism. By practicing the contemplative exercises of this level, we become aware of our mind and our five senses. At this level, we continue to be conscious of our body and the interaction between the body and thoughts and develop an inner and outer sensory-perceptive contemplation. We become aware of the movement, gravity, and space around us.

After the first level, where we observed the positive sensations and emotions in the body felt in the present time, *now,* at this level, we can imagine a *future* containing more of these experiences. We move towards taking a positive vision, focusing on future goals, projects, events, and we become deeply aware of the structures and functions of our minds, senses, and muscles.

LEVEL THREE (SDR 3) is inspired by Zen. The meditative exercises are built on the concepts of levels one and two, and now, with the eyes partly open, we become aware of the interaction between our mind and body, and also of the world around us.

Once we have reinforced our mental and physical structures by noticing the joy and happiness in the present and the future, we are ready to investigate the beautiful moments from the *past.* Our consciousness is oriented at this level more towards what is outside of us, but we move between the inner and the outer world perceiving both as if for the first time. At this level, we meditate both sitting and walking. We also go deeper into our body becoming aware of our bones.

> *The main focus at this level is on*
> *the mind-body-emotions relationship,*
> *past time, meditation,*
> *and activating the cell structures*
> *of the bones.*

LEVEL FOUR (SDR4). Based on the experience and the insights acquired in the first three levels, Dr. Caycedo emphasizes the importance of being aware of and knowing our needs and values.

This level also includes all the concepts already learned. We began to focus our attention on the inner world, then exploring and contemplating the outer world, arriving at this level where "all is one". The past, present and future, all captured in the present moment. Awareness is internal and external as we experience contemplative movement through time and space.

Our attention also focuses on the kinesthetic sensations (the capacity to perceive the movement of different parts of the body) and cenesthetic (internal awareness of bodily existence caused by the internal sensations).

At this level, we become aware of our internal organs, our needs and values, discovering at the same time the three dimensions of time (past, present and future) and space.

> *The main focus at this level is on personal values,*
> *the dimension of space and time,*
> *activating the cell structure of the vital organs,*
> *and on existential values, liberty,*
> *responsibility and dignity.*

The 2nd cycle – Radical

Having discovered and reinforced our mental and physical structures during the first cycle, we now begin to discover our place in the universe. At this stage, we become aware of the energy and vibration of our body, of phylogenesis (the history of the species) and ontogenesis (the development and transformation of the body to the adult form).

Here we ask "radical questions" such as "Who am I?", "Why am I here?", "What is life?" and develop our intuition.

> *The main focus is on the awareness*
> *of the different vibrations*
> *of the body and the voice.*

The 3rd cycle – Existential

During this cycle, our knowledge and consciousness expand, and we start practicing a new form of existence. We live in full awareness, understanding the *sophronic consciousness,* and we become fully aware of the connectedness of the universe. Everything is seen from a new perspective.

> *In this cycle we strengthen*
> *the existential human values:*
> *freedom, responsibility,*
> *and dignity.*

The four principles of sophrology

1. POSITIVE ACTION, which means to reinvigorate and activate what is positive in us. It is a process through which every positive conscious action has positive repercussions on the whole being, at all levels: cognitive, emotional, behavioral, and spiritual.

In sophrology, positive means every intrinsic benefic force (*valence*) that supports and encourages the attainment of sophronic consciousness – smooth and lucid by a person. We can achieve this kind of awareness by energizing and consolidating the positive structures and intrinsic powers in us, which are feelings, sensations, thoughts, memories, and positive attitudes towards ourselves and our existence.

Focusing on the negative aspects of life, sickness, pain, or symptoms, makes us forget about the positive and about our health, and locks us into a *pathological consciousness*.

2. CORPORALITY (BODY) AS LIVING REALITY, represents the foundation of sophrology exercises. It is about the way we perceive our body, the reality of our body. During the exercises, we become more and more familiar with our body, gradually attaining more profound levels. If initially we learn to perceive its shape, its temperature, and its size, later we develop an awareness of its cells, muscles, bones, and internal

organs. In this way, we bring the mind "home", to the present time.

3. THE PRINCIPLE OF OBJECTIVE REALITY. This concept means to keep an objective attitude, that is a perception of what is there and not what we think is there, being non-judgmental, with an open and curious mind, accepting things just the way they are in that moment.

We talk about the subjective when we distort our perception of things. Consciousness can be more or less subjective, depending on the degree of stability of a person. Sophrology proposes that we balance our consciousness and perceive reality and things as they are.

4. ADAPTABILITY, which means that all the techniques and theories of sophrology are adapted to the reality of the client. These fundamental principles represent the basic elements of the sophronic consciousness.

The pillars of sophrology

The official recognition of sophrology as a scientific discipline is based on the following three concepts:

1. A clear and coherent <u>epistemology</u>. Epistemology studies the process of knowledge as it unfolds in science; the theory behind scientific knowledge, its presuppositions, and foundations. The theories explaining sophrologic discipline were developed by Dr. Caycedo and are based on phenomenological investigation.

2. <u>A methodology</u> of its own, meaning all the methods we use. The structure, the set of practices, exercises, and rules used in sophrology, Sophro Dynamic Relaxation, and the associated techniques.

3. A specific <u>semantic</u> that is the meaning of words from the descriptive, comparative, and especially historical point of view. The words we use in sophrology and their sense, the descriptions of the terms used (corporality, vivance, terpnos logos, pheno-description, sophroliminal level).

The states and levels of consciousness

Dr. Caycedo talks about awareness as a set of intrapersonal and interpersonal realities and says that states of consciousness represent qualitative changes between sickness and total health. For a better visual understanding, please examine the graphic from page 52.

THE PATHOLOGICAL STATE OF CONSCIOUSNESS (PC). Here the consciousness is veiled and disintegrated. This psychological state is predominant in people touched by disease or various daily conditions (physical or mental such as back pain, headache, malaise, a slight depression, or other common everyday illnesses) and extends to those who are suffering from severe depression, hysteria, schizophrenia, or irreversible mental deterioration. Pathological consciousness is studied by medicine, psychiatry, and psychopathology.

THE ORDINARY (COMMON) STATE OF CONSCIOUSNESS (OC) is also veiled and disintegrated but to a lesser extent and is present in those who live entirely according to pre-established patterns and make use of mental representations accepted from society, without questioning and without looking at things anew. The characteristic of this state of consciousness is that people think their negative feelings or emotions are the fault of others and live in the "unconscious" without realizing that they can choose their thoughts and emotions and that they are responsible for their life. The ordinary consciousness is studied by general psychology.

THE SOPHRONIC STATE OF CONSCIOUSNESS (SC) is studied by sophrology. In this state, consciousness is illuminated from the inside out and entails a positive existential integration. This means to access a body-mind-spirit harmony. People living in this way realize they are responsible for their emotions, their actions, and their way of being, and become co-creators of their lives, following their existence with dignity, liberty, and responsibility. These people become *conscious of their consciousness* and therefore are no longer able to live unconsciously. This does not mean that what happens to them in life is always wonderful, amazing, or fantastic. The sophronic state of consciousness does not preclude illness, accidents, or disasters but a person living in this state will see these events in a very different manner from a person who is in the common state of consciousness or a pathological state of consciousness.

According to Dr. Caycedo, human consciousness is "veiled" because our focus is mainly oriented towards the outside world, and our inner world is unknown to us. Our existence is dictated by programming and instincts, and only through a contemplative or meditative method, we can "discover" the consciousness.

Consciousness is a force responsible for integrating all the structures of human existence. And it's not just an awareness of internal and external realities, but a cohesive force that integrates body, mind, and all the structures responsible for the existence of human beings.

Consciousness is a mental process, thoughts, feelings or perceptions that we are aware of, so it urges us to think about what we are thinking of, a self-awareness. It is the feeling of understanding personal existence, the most advanced way of being human. Consciousness is also the feeling that man has over the morality of his actions.

Consciousness and awareness are two terms that are intertwined, expressing a superior form of thought. It is an elevated form of living, the fullness of one's existence, man's capacity to realize that he exists.

To be conscious means to be attentive, to observe, to be with the mind in present, to be awake and aware – the opposite of being "unconscious".

When we start sophrology exercises we are in the *awake* level, most of us being in the common state of consciousness. By doing the basic sophronisation,

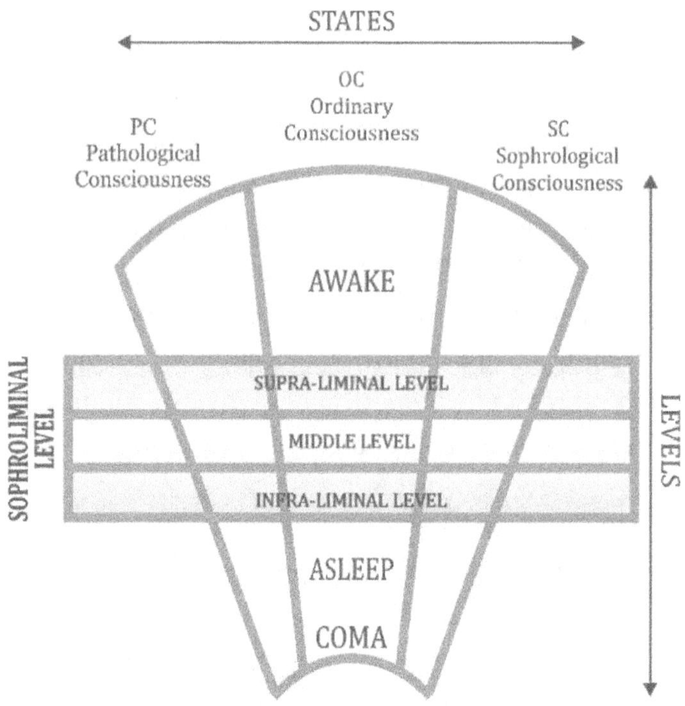

we move into the *sophroliminal* levels. Then we do one of the sophrology exercises (intra-sophronic activation), and after we end the exercise (de-sophronisation), we move up to the awake level again, having progressed towards a sophronic state of consciousness (SC).

The levels of consciousness have also a few characteristics, correlated with the intensity of awareness.

The AWAKE LEVEL. There are many ways of being awake, some more conscious than others. In general, this is an active state of being. The attention gravitates toward the external world seeking to live it in a clear, organized, and realistic manner.

Between the awake level and sleep, we have the SOPHROLIMINAL LEVELS, those in which we practice sophrology exercises:

- The upper level, supra-liminal, corresponds to an activation of consciousness, as for example are Zen exercises;
- The middle level integrates and balances consciousness. During the sophrology exercises we work mainly in this level. In sophrology we do not alter consciousness. The consciousness is becoming aware of itself as it is, without judgment and with curiosity and wonder. Here the consciousness illuminates itself (becomes aware of itself);
- The lower level, named infra-liminal, corresponds to an inhibition of consciousness, for example hypnosis, pharmacology (classification and therapeutic action of drugs), trance, or certain states of yoga.

SLEEP. During sleep, our body goes through several cycles, and wakefulness is lost. The two states (awake-sleep) alternate in our life, and their coordination is ensured by complex brain processes. During sleep, the state of consciousness is replaced by a state of unconsciousness. The process is reversible, so the sensory stimulation brings us back to a waking and conscious state.

COMA is a prolonged state of unconsciousness including a lack of response to stimuli, from which it is impossible to rouse a person.

*

Achieving and maintaining a sophronic state of consciousness is the aim of sophrology. Every one of us can attain sophronic consciousness in certain moments of "connectedness", for example when we have a great idea, when we create, when we admire a work art, when we are connected with nature, when we love. The goal is to live in this state as much as possible.

"Without judgment", "as if it is for the first time", "with curiosity and wonder", are very important concepts for staying in a sophronic state of consciousness, therefore we have to maintain them active all the time in our mind.

The five systems and the mega system

All sophrological exercises and theories are closely related to the physical body and to the intimate connection we have with our bodies. To better understand Sophro-Dynamic Relaxation, we need to know that it takes into consideration five major "systems", plus the mega system (the whole body).

The five systems are parts of the body divided according to the concentration of nerves in certain points of the body. These systems follow the neural plexus in the body. There are five nerve plexuses that transport information to and from each of these systems. The sixth system is the whole body.

When we concentrate our attention on smaller parts of the body, we notice the physical sensations more easily and in more detail than when we focus on the whole body at once. In addition, since the nerves transmit these sensations, we can actually feel the back of the arms and the palms separately from the front of the arms and hands. During the exercises, we move our attention up or down in the body, focusing on the information given by each of these major nerve plexus.

Each system has a point of integration in its center. Behind every point there are endocrine glands. The further we advance in the sophrologic training, the more complex and focused the exercises are. We discover our six systems which, as can be seen in the figure on the next page, are divided as follows:

FIRST SYSTEM – head, brain, eyes, nose, ears, mouth and jaw, hypothalamus, pituitary, and pineal glands. Integration point – middle of forehead.

SECOND SYSTEM – neck, throat, shoulders, the outside part of the arms, hands and fingers, thyroid, and parathyroid glands. Integration point – middle of neck.

THIRD SYSTEM – the chest, upper back, the underside of the arms, palms of the hands, fingers, and thymus gland. Integration point – middle of chest.

FOURTH SYSTEM – area between the chest and the navel, the middle of the back, internal organs, adrenalin glands, and pancreas. Integration point – midway between navel and solar plexus.

FIFTH SYSTEM – lower abdomen, lower back, hips, legs, feet and toes, testicles, and ovaries. Integration point – just below the navel.

SIXTH SYSTEM – the whole body, the endocrine system. Integration point – the navel.

Those who are familiar with Eastern medicine, will already have made the connection between these systems, the nerve plexus, and the chakras. The missing ones are the link with the universe from the top of the head, and the link with the earth from the base of the body.

We do not use the word chakra in sophrology, since sophrology is all about putting previously held ideas and beliefs aside for the moment and discovering what is *there*. So the word "system" is used because it is neutral and most people will be unaware of the context, and so they have no preconceptions and are open to discover what is *there*.

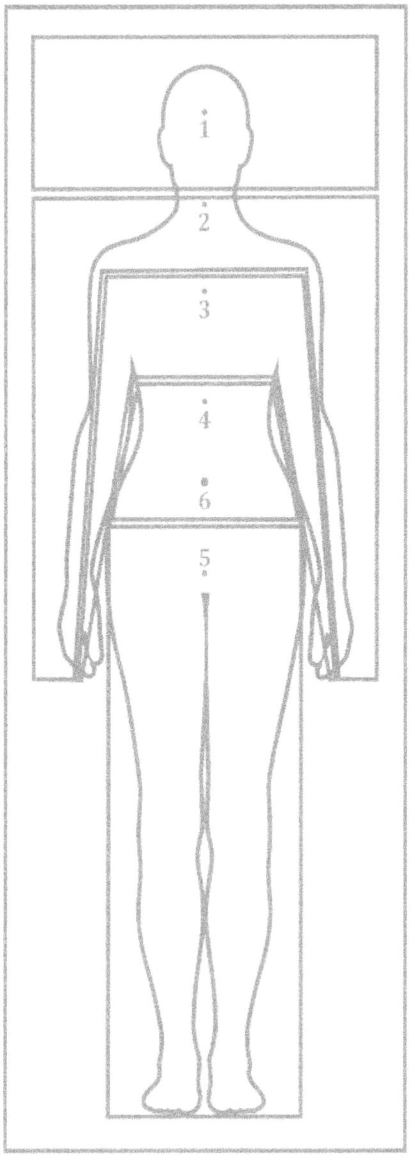

If we use the word chakra, people may start with some beliefs or ideas about what a chakra is.

The vivance

The theory of *vivential process of being* is the theory of transformation of mind and body, which takes place with the repeated practice of the SDRs and their related techniques.

The word "vivance" comes from Spanish, "vivencia", and it is a word that is part of the language of sophrology. The German term is "erlebnis". It means to become aware of what we are aware of but the word vivance is more than a simple experience. We become aware of our *intentionality*[5], which means bringing into conscious what was previously formed in the unconscious, to observe what we are focusing on, at each moment. This awareness could be through any of the senses. Our consciousness is always conscious of something. When we notice what that is, we produce a vivance. It is almost like giving a name to, defining, and noticing what is there, a moment in which the mind or consciousness perceives a new sensation.

Each vivance arising from each vivencial experience produces a vivance that, when recognized, is like a light being turned on in consciousness.

---

[5] Concept taken from phenomenology. More details on page 66.

Every time we discover a new vivance, we notice something we didn't realize existed. Once we notice this new sensation, we cannot say that we do not know it. It comes to light. We have many parts that are visible, and others which are invisible. As we do the exercises, more and more sensations come to light, and our body becomes lighter.

By repeating the exercises and continually discover vivances, we start to feel changes in three stages:

Discovery

Mastery

Transformation.

The exercises are more effective if they are short and repeated frequently, even for just 10 minutes. After each sophrology session, the client is asked to repeat the exercise, either by listening to a recording, or by repeating it mentally. Mastery of sophronic consciousness does not just appear naturally, it requires perseverance and regular practice, just like anything else we learn (sport, a foreign language, dancing). Awareness of the vivance and talking or writing about them in our *pheno-description*[6] journal, speeds up the learning process.

---

[6] What you have experienced during the exercises. Description of phenomena (sensations, perceptions, feelings) that you have noticed in your body.

All sophrological exercises and techniques are vivencial processes through which we guide our consciousness towards good experiences, pleasurable, and agreeable physical sensations. This process leads us gradually towards sophrological consciousness.

We can, of course, live a different vivencial process, and guide our attention and consciousness towards unpleasant experiences, and note these vivances and their effect on our body, but that process leads us gradually towards the pathological consciousness. Our aim is to feel good, to train our mind to notice pleasant things, to direct our attention toward pleasure and joy, and to notice their positive effect on our body.

The structures of consciousness

According to sophrology, consciousness is constituted by several phronic structures, which encompass the dynamic integration of being. The phronic structures are graphically shown in the figure on the page 62, named "The sophrology cup".

In sophrology, the consciousness can be interpreted as energy containing "positive", "negative", "neutral", and "silent" charges, called *phronic structures*. These are explained in the following manner:

1. The VALENCES are the smallest elements of the consciousness and we have:
- Positive valances "+" (sophronic), which are pleasant thoughts, memories, experiences, or emotions;
- Negative valences "-" (anaphronic), are unpleasant thoughts, memories, experiences, or emotions;
- Neutral valences "n", comprise indifferent information, neither pleasant nor unpleasant;
- Silent or muted valences "s", are the biological information stored in the body, hidden from the awareness.

2. PHRONIC UNIT (OR PHRONIC CELL). Units or cells are made up of several valences, like atoms and molecules (two or more atoms form a molecule). Several positive valences together lead to a healthily functioning of mind and body. Several negative valences together lead to an unhealthily functioning of mind and body.

3. STRUCTURES. Millions of units (groups of valences) together, form structures, which create our "worlds":

– *Present structures* create *the world of present phenomena,* and represent the things observable in present time, what we are conscious of. Things we know that we know. The present structures are also related to the external world, the valences we assimilated from our family, teachers, society, media, social networks, politics, and religion.

According to what we received from outside, we gathered plus, minus, or neutral valences ("You are good", "You are stupid"...). This world is also related to the way we express ourselves outwardly as our behavior or code of conduct and here we can see clearly which our values are, and we can look at the results of our decisions.

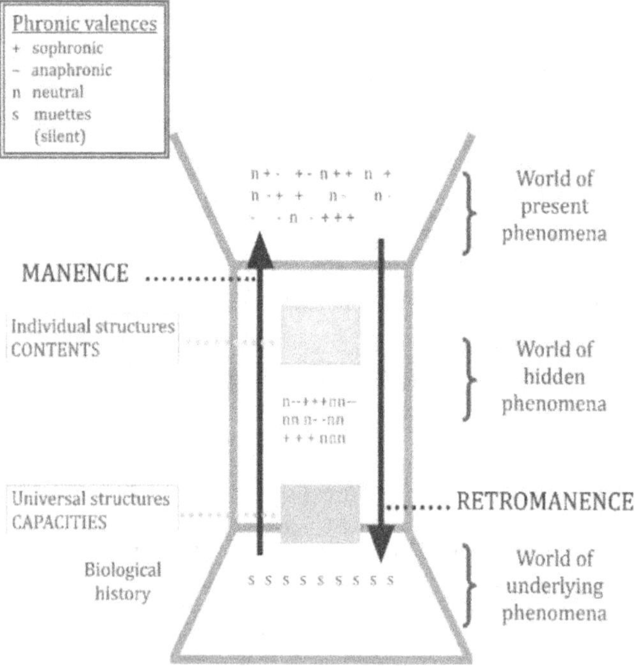

– *Latent structures* create *the world of latent phenomena* and represent the hidden, unrevealed phenomena that are about to emerge. These are things we are unconscious of but that we can access. Things we know that we don't know. In the world of latent phenomena, we have plus valences, which encourage us, and minus valences, which discourage us. These are the things we accept as truths, ideas in which we believe ("I'm not creative", "I'm beautiful", "I'm clumsy", "Those like me do like that..."), beliefs, habits and attitudes – all these become our "programs". We believe in them and they work.

– *Underlying structures* create *the world of underlying phenomena,* and are represented by biological phenomena, structures expressed by our biology and our body. These unconscious structures act without being under our conscious control, for example ontogenesis - the changes of the body from the embryo stage until the end of its existence, phylogenesis - the development of life on earth, biology, the anatomic and physiologic manifestations, the genetic reservoir, and the individual essence.

The latent and underlying structures possess all that is needed for transformation. The phronic structures represent all the human potential. Sophrology works on this potential by activating the positive units within the latent structures. This results in an increased integration of the consciousness and a healthier human being.

The impact of positive actions (principle of positive action) on the phronic unit (group of valences), results in an increase in positive units.

The dynamic integration of being

Every morning when we wake up, we move from the fundamental and latent worlds into the conscious world. When we go to sleep, we do the opposite. During the night, we integrate all that we have experienced during the day. During the day, we experience life, and during the night, we integrate our experiences.

We use this natural mechanism of consciousness in sophrology. We notice the phenomena that arise from the underlying and latent areas into consciousness by doing dynamic exercises, and then we integrate during the phronic pauses the phenomena and the experiences that we have brought into consciousness. Gradually, our consciousness and our life force grow and expand.

If we look back at "The sophrology cup", we can understand more easily the objective of sophrology training, whose aim is to put negative valences *in brackets* (during the session) and to increase the number of positive valences of our consciousness (which supports us in our daily life). In this way, we positively energize our latent and underlying world. This process is called *retromanence* (the arrow pointing down), which descends and brings then into the conscious world and into our present existence capacities and positive valences through a forward movement, called manence (the arrow pointing up).

In other words, during sophrology exercises, we go down to the depths of our being and consciousness, retromanence, and the manence is what emerges from this depth (e.g. reviving a capacity), we bring something new into the light. This movement in the hidden worlds of our being is positively oriented, and it is active during sophrology sessions.

THE CAPACITIES AND CONTENTS OF THE CONSCIOUSNESS are two different concepts in the theory of sophrology. These are situated ***in the world of latent phenomena***. *The contents* are individual and personal (e.g. memories) and *the capacities* are universal (e.g. memory).

Dr. Caycedo proposes a non-exhaustive list of 31 capacities present in each one of us, which we all develop differently. In sophrology, we work with these structures in order to become more aware of how we are using them, and how to improve and strengthen them.

All these capacities are structures existing in us:

1. Rhythm of sleep, 2. Corporality (body) as living reality, 3. Cenesthesia, 4. Kinesthesia, 5. Sensations (the five senses), 6. Perception (the capture and interpretation of sensations), 7. Feelings, 8. Memory, 9. Orientation, 10. Thoughts, 11. Attention, 12. Concentration, 13. Contemplation, 14. Association, 15. Language, 16. Intelligence, 17. Learning, 18.Communication, 19. Sexuality, 20. Conservation, 21. Imagination, 22. Emotion, 23. Affectivity, 24. Transformation, 25. Sociability, 26. Futurisation (means to project ourselves in future, taking into consideration our positive existential potential), 27. Understanding, 28. Rationalization, 29. Reflection, 30. Will-power, 31. Moral conscience.

Intention and intentionality

Being based on the discipline of phenomenology, sophrology uses the concepts of *intention* and *intentionality*. Consciousness is always conscious of something, and that something is not an accident.

Intentionality is what we automatically focus on (or notice) every moment of the day. What we notice depends on two things:

1. What is of value to us.

2. What is a threat and danger to us.

For example, if we are an artist, we will automatically notice colors, shapes and forms. If we love nature and plants, we will notice flowers and plants wherever we go. If someone represents a threat, we will notice things associated with that person.

Intention is something we want to do, we intend something, it is our personal will to concentrate our attention in a certain direction. Intentionality "drags" attention to where attention falls without us paying attention to it. Attention falls automatically without us being conscious of what is happening.

When we become aware of our intentionality, we bring to the surface, in our consciousness, thoughts, beliefs, attitudes, and values that "conduct" our life, the unconscious "programs". And because we want to live in a conscious way, not run by these programs, becoming aware of them is what we can do to have a more fulfilling life and more fulfilling experiences.

Every thought sends a neurological impulse through our entire body that either strengthens us or weakens us. The power we have comes from studying, understanding, and immersing ourselves in that which bring us power, and in avoiding that which weakens us.

The Phronic Region

The "Black Box" or the "hexagon of consciousness", symbolizes ordinary consciousness. The hexagon is divided in four parts (present, past, future, totalisation) and it is closed, it doesn't have any space, the world is seen as pre-established.

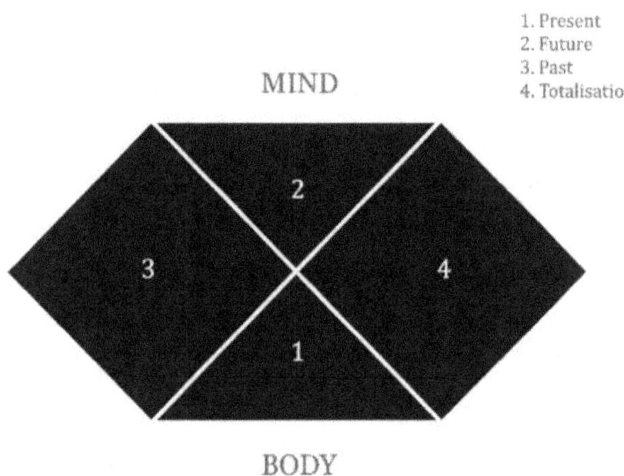

Through the regular practice of the Reductive Cycle, consciousness illuminates itself from inside, becoming the Phronic Region, symbolically represented by the figure at page 70. In sophrology, we construct this new space, a new phenomenological territory , where we become aware of the three temporal dimensions, present, future and past, included in the whole (all is one) – totalization. We become also fully aware of the dimensions of time and space, in each moment. When we are fully present, we transform our old way of being because the Black Box opens as we do the exercises and makes space for progressively creating the Phronic Region, full of light. In this space, the mind and the body establish a phenomenological relationship. This region takes shape and comes into existence from the associations of millions of interconnections within our cerebral fibers, thanks to the energy of our consciousness. The region is formed by regular sophrology practice. The potential for creating this region exists in each one of us. Through practice, we progressively integrate the vivances from the life inside of us by becoming aware of our contents (sensations, emotions, feelings, views, habits, beliefs, memories, judgments), and the process leads us to a new way of experiencing the world.

"Sophrology cannot exist without the Phronic Region concept, in the same way that psychoanalysis can't exist without the concept of unconsciousness. The final outcome of the Reductive Cycle is the discovery of the Phronic Region." Dr. Alfonso Caycedo, Dorna Revie - *Practicioner Diploma Course.*

So, the phronic structures of consciousness are discovered when practicing the Radical Cycle and become apparent through the Phronic Region. Without this awareness of body-mind relationship (the construction of the Phronic Region), consciousness is chaotic, ordinary and diverted. The Region is therefore, a space in which to exist. At the beginning it is "closed", but gradually, as we reinforce our structures in the Radical Cycle of sophrology, the Region "lights up".

Terpnos Logos

This term comes from Greek language and groups together the tone, the voice, the intensity, and the language used by sophrologist to guide the exercises. The sophrologist adopts a familiar and relaxed tone, and the voice should reverberate from inside, to profoundly resonate with his/her own body.

The terpnos logos can be: informative (specific and detailed descriptions and visualizations), persuasive (more hypnotic, strongly guiding and leading the client), orientative (a neutral and open language, so that the clients follow their own sensations, thoughts and feelings in order that the phenomena arising be as pure as possible). This is the most frequently used language in sophrology. It is often said that silence is the best terpnos logos for sophrology, therefore we use as few words as possible.

Sophronic alliance

The sophronic alliance describes the specific relationship between the sophrologist and the client. This is a special relationship, of mutual development and respect, in real time, both conscious of the phenomena and the interaction taking place.

The sophrologist accompanies the clients, focusing on their needs, whether therapeutical or personal development, with openness and under-standing, and without judgment. This attitude is one of the fundamental concepts of sophrology, therefore the client is encouraged to adopt the same attitude not just during the exercises, but also in everyday life, both in the relationship with herself/himself and with others.

All sophrologists practice all the techniques during their training, integrating the benefits at the individual level, and then transmitting them in a therapeutic and preventive way.

The sophrologist has a positive attitude, open, paying attention to the client (to their body language, their way of expressing, and other perceptions), listens, avoiding interference from his/her own judgments or interpretations (phenomenological attitude), in order to guide the therapy in a harmonious way. The client becomes involved in his own development and the sophrologist encourages the autonomy of the client (the clients can practice alone the exercises after they have assimilated the attitudes and the sophrological exercises).

The applications of sophrology

Health

Sophrology was born in the medical field, as a unique or complementary therapy, depending on the patient, diagnosis, or other particulars of their situation. Dr. Caycedo said that the patient is taught to discover their consciousness and to move from pathological consciousness to the sophronic consciousness (harmonious). There are many doctors, psychiatrists, psychologists, physiotherapists, and nurses who practice the sophrological method in Europe. Individual sophrologic treatment is used as a therapeutic or preventive method for various conditions:

- Mental discomfort such as anxiety, stress, irritability, overwork, insomnia, psychosomatic disorders, eating disorders, or physical changes that affect the mental state etc.;
- Physical problems. For people in physical rehabilitation, sophrology reactivates some functions which have been reduced as a consequence of pathological processes, for example, certain treatment is combined with sophrology. Often, the circulatory system (heart) and the respiratory system (lungs) are involved in the biggest psychosomatic problems. Chest pain, palpitations, tachycardia,

and hyperventilation are common symptoms in stressed and anxious patients. Through sophrology, the person learns to control their tension, and thus, these tensions diminish or disappear;

- Existential difficulties. Life's special circumstances that require sophrological support in overcoming moments as the management of change and transition, grief, and chronic fatigue.

Sophrology is one from the most commonly used methods in preparing for childbirth in France and in other French and Spanish speaking countries, and it is becoming more and more popular in England. Sophrology helps women to fully enjoy their pregnancy, to be aware and accept the changes taking place during this period. The result of exercises is a decrease in worries related to the pregnancy, and women learn to relax, to be calm and confident.

Even though sophrology began in the medical field, its application has been extended into other domains as well.

Sport

As mentioned in the presentation of the brief history, sophrology has had an important role and impressive results in the sporting area.

Athletes train both physically and technically to achieve excellent performance. Sophrology complements the traditional approach, adding up a mental and emotional preparation that revives the positive capacities of the body and encouraging bodily awareness, corporality, and sensoriality. The specific exercises help athletes stay calm and focused during competitions and to have an alert mind and precise movements. Its effectiveness has been demonstrated by many Swiss champions who have won more than 200 medals in the last 20 years[7].

Learning to be totally present, to dissipate unwanted fears and thoughts, athletes activate their potential, successfully channeling all their energy.

Education

Sophrology is a science that believes in human potential from an educational point of view. It develops and strengthens individual capacities, focuses on positive experiences and vivances in the body, helping young people to be confident in their abilities, to be autonomous, free, and safe in terms of their thoughts and actions.

Students and pupils can learn sophrologic techniques in order to know their bodies and mental states better, actively participating in their intellectual and personal development. At the intellectual level,

---

[7] www.sofrologia.com

there are exercises to develop attention, concentration, and memory, and on a personal level, by working on how the student approaches and reacts to certain events and situations related to school, university, work, family, friends, and colleagues, learning to control situations that generate stress.

The exercises bring more calmness and lucidity to the life of students and pupils, especially at times when they need to prepare intensively for exams. With practice, they tend to be more relaxed and have more confidence in themselves. It is never too early for them to learn to relax, to acquire a positive attitude towards life, to develop harmoniously, and to be serene.

Business

Sometimes, the balance between work, family and leisure is not easy to maintain. Work has an important role in our lives, often occupying more than eight hours a day. For busy and active people, the regular practice of sophrology results in greater calmness and improved relaxation, reducing the risk of professional exhaustion (burnout syndrome).

CHAPTER THREE

Sophrology
practice and exercises

Sophrology attitudes

This chapter describes how the sophrology practice unfolds. To make it easy to understand, I chose some exercises we usually use at the beginning, and I explained each step and what it means. I also share with you a few pheno-descriptions of my clients, the response which emerged during the sophrology sessions.

Before we move to the actual explanation of how an exercise unfolds, I must mention the appropriate attitudes to have when we practice sophrology. These attitudes come from phenomenology, and if we use them in daily life, we become more open, flexible, and resilient, we learn to accept others and ourselves easier and to judge less. Besides the health benefits, you will see an improvement in the quality of the interior life (you with yourself) and the relationships with others, so we can say that sophrology is an adventure that leads to the discovery of the self and the others.

1. WE SUSPEND JUDGEMENT, preconceived ideas, and we accept what is there. We become aware of our thoughts and note that it is a personal opinion and not reality.

Through *judgment* we create our own version of reality, we invent our own story about reality. Leaving judgments aside, we are more open mentally, we do not "feel obliged" to label. Preconceptions limit us, narrowing our horizons. Acceptance frees us and helps us to suspend judgment, seeing and experiencing reality as it is.

We can do the same with people: instead of thinking in terms of "I like/I don't like" somebody, we can leave our mind free to discover the person, we can focus on the qualities and not on the defects, and on what is beautiful and good in a person. Is there anybody that can say about himself that he is perfect? We don't know how we "look" in the eyes of others. If we ask different people how they perceive us, we will see that the answers vary, and what is more, we can find ourselves surprised by what we hear. Reality is based on perceptions. Why should we project our own perceptions onto others?

2. AS IF IT IS FOR THE FIRST TIME. During the exercises, we explore our bodies with this attitude in mind. Seeing things, situations, and persons as if it is for the first time, we are open to seeing new possibilities, to seeing the world and circumstances from a new perspective.

As if for the first time, with curiosity and wonder! As we would unwrap a beautifully wrapped gift, smiling, we don't know what we will find inside but we know it's beautiful, and that joy encourages us to discover it, full of curiosity and emotion. What if we look at the following day as though it were an extraordinary gift that we receive every day? This is the inner attitude that produces change, which leads us to look at things differently, with openness, putting everything in a new light or color.

Or you can observe the route you take to your job, that you follow every day but which you don't really notice, as if you are seeing it for the first time. Use the same attitude you have whenever you visit a new place. Notice what happens in your body when you do this.

Or friends and family members that you have known for years watch them as if you are seeing them for the first time, try to consider them, full of curiosity, as with the previously mentioned gift. Try the same with colleagues, your office or the house you live in.

This attitude, adopted permanently, produces changes in our mind and body because it maintains our energy in the present and opens up new opportunities to experience the fullness of reality.

3. WE PUT IN "BRACKETS". We put everything we know or have learned up until now aside, along

with all our worries and preoccupations. In this way, we are open to fully experience what happens during the exercise. Our minds are ready and free to learn and explore, we are present physically and mentally.

4. WE REPEAT THE EXERCISES REGULARLY to produce long lasting changes. We practice the sophrology exercises to integrate new ways of mental functioning into everyday life, creating new neural circuits due to the plasticity of the brain. Neuroplasticity is the potential which the brain has to reorganize itself through the creation of new circuits, a malleability that help us to adapt to our needs and to the constant changing world.

The brain can reshape at any age. Every moment of the day, changes in our brain generated by what happens to us, by emotions and thoughts take place. When neurons are activated at the same time as a reaction to certain stimuli, they interconnect, creating strong connections. The more we practice something, the more the connections are strengthened and become stronger. And the opposite is true. If we want to get rid of a habit and we suddenly stop doing it, the connections fade away and it's going to be more and more difficult for us to do it. In sophrology, when we learn something new or try to overcome a habit that no longer serves us, we focus on building new neural pathways by repeating sophrology exercises and techniques, knowing that the more we focus and practice something, the better we become at the new skill that we are learning.

During the exercises, numerous neural changes take place because the brain is engaged. In this way, we can eliminate old deep-rooted beliefs, ideas and old habits that are no longer useful.

What happens during an exercise?

During the exercises, we become aware of our body, observing with curiosity and wonder the physical sensations and phenomena that arise. A sophrologic approach starts by acknowledging our corporality and reintegrating this primordial function in the present. In order to turn our attention inwards, we have to eliminate external distractions. A good way to remove them is to close our receptors, especially sight and hearing. For sight it is easy, we just have to close our eyes. Hearing is more difficult, but we will have to mentally close ourselves off from external noise so that we can hear our inner sounds. Focusing requires an effort of will and constitutes an excellent opportunity for development.

The objective is to make someone responsible and autonomous, to be able to live an authentic life. What matters is doing the exercises; these are many and various, and for the purpose of presenting the steps we use in sophrology, I have chosen one that is very effective in eliminating physical tensions.

Sophro-Relaxation-Release

PRE-SOPHRONIC INFORMATION contains an explanation of the session, the objectives, and the method:

This exercise is called Sophro-Relaxation-Release (the short version).

It is a simple method used to get rid of all the negative sensations and emotions generated by the body, a kind of spring cleaning of the body.

It is also a very good exercise for people who are going through a difficult period. Breathing out any pain or suffering from both the physical and mental planes, has positive consequences for all the structures of consciousness. Pain is always mental and physical, always fused together. The reality is that a person is living this phenomenon, this pain. This exercise helps us to get rid of the pain, not by attacking the cause but by changing the way in which the person experiences the pain.

You will become aware of the whole body, as if for the first time, exploring it with curiosity from top to bottom. I will name each part of the body, and I just want you to notice it. It may help you to imagine that you are a

BASIC SOPHRONISATION it is the process by which the sophrologist guides the client to discover his body. Generally, when we notice what is *there*, the body relaxes automatically. The aim is not to relax the body but to become aware of the body and accept it as it is at every moment. Usually, after basic sophronisation, the client is more relaxed. Initially, some people will probably reach the supra-liminal level, but with training, the body will gain more confidence and will move to the middle level. Others relax more easily and connect quickly with their body:

Close your eyes so you can concentrate better on what is happening inside. If the eyes are open, you can be distracted more easily, but if you prefer to stay with your eyes open, that is fine too.

Become aware of your body as if it is for the first time...
become aware of sounds outside the room... the sounds inside the room...
and of the sounds of your own body, breathing... heart beat...
welcome these sounds as being part of life, without trying to work out what they are...

now focus on your head, and become aware of all the sensations...
especially of your forehead, eyes, muscles around your eyes... nose, the air going in and the air going out...
everything that happens in and out of the ears...
jaw and mouth...
and back of the head...
move your attention down to the neck and throat...
observing everything that happens in the shoulders, the outside part of the arms, elbow, wrist, hand and fingers, all the phenomena that arise...

INTRA-SOPHRONIC ACTIVATION. After we have completed the basic sophronisation exercise and we have become aware of the body, we continue with the chosen method, in this case tension release:

Breathe out fully emptying the stomach and lungs...

breathe in deeply, hold your breath, bring your hands above your head and tense the whole body...

the face, throat, shoulders, abdomen, buttocks, legs, all the muscles...

a bit more...

and at the same time notice the sensations arising from the accumulated tensions...

hold a little bit more...

and exhale releasing, put your hands down...

with each out breath release all tensions...

with each out breath release the physical, emotional and mental tensions...

breath out again fully emptying the stomach and lungs...

breath in deeply, hold your breath, bring your hands above your head and tense the whole body...

face, throat, shoulders, abdomen, buttocks, legs, all the muscles...

more...

and at the same time notice the sensations coming from the accumulated tensions...

then exhale again, releasing all the tensions in the body with each out breath...

and for the third time exhale, inhale, tense the whole body...

hold a little bit more...

notice all the arising phenomena with curiosity...

and then release with each out breath...

THE INTEGRATION PAUSE is an important moment during the exercise, which allows us to integrate, to observe, and assimilate the sensations offered by the body. Once conscious effort gradually diminishes, a new world unfolds, our inner universe, accompanied by the deep whispers of our being, of life:

Let yourself be carried away by this kind of pleasant feeling of calmness and quietness, this inner rearrangement, an intimate communication with your body...

all the physical sensations are welcome, observe them with curiosity and wonder...

notice also how you body feels now.

DE-SOPHRONISATION marks the end of the exercise, returning to the general tonus demanded by everyday life, and returning to normal alertness, but one step closer to the sophronic state of consciousness. Gently and gradually we move our body, from the bottom-up, we stretch and we open our eyes only

when we are ready when we are sure that we've fully
recovered both the tonus and alertness.

THE POST-SOPHRONIC DIALOG (interaction with
the sophrologist) is very important, because if we do
not express what we felt during the exercise, these
feelings may remain deep inside our body, and we
don't really take advantage of them while expressing
them orally or writing them down will ensure we
retain the benefits.

These realizations are called *pheno-descriptions*.
The pheno-descriptions are new vivances – feelings
and sensations we experienced during the exercises. If
you do the sophrological exercises on your own and
you don't have the opportunity to talk with a
sophrologist, writing down your pheno-descriptions
increases the process of awareness; writing in a
journal helps us remember what we felt, in which part
of the body, not just having a vague feeling of "It was
good", "I feel at peace", "Relaxing", "I'm more calm", "I
don't feel so tense anymore"... We tend to forget or not

to put any emphasis on the sensations we receive from our body and through sophrology practice we want to be one and in harmony with our body. Writing in a journal helps us train our minds to pay attention to the sensations we experience during the exercises, so that we live more and more consciously in our everyday life. At the same time, becoming aware of these phenomena and discussing them with the sophrologist, can have a profound therapeutic effect.

Below are some pheno-descriptions written by my clients. Remember that everyone feels, becomes aware and describes in his own way. Phenodescriptions are personal, a result of an intimate interaction with our own body. Each time may be different, even if we practice the same exercise, and the experience may not be the same for everybody:

"Now I'm more relaxed and cheerful.
After tension and experiencing relief in my body, I feel lighter. I perceived a pleasant sensation of warmth in the abdominal area."

"It was a new and unique feeling, being the first time that I have done this kind of exercise. I was happy to meet my physical body in this way. It was
somehow a visualization, an exploration of it from inside, that is I didn't try to detach myself imaginatively from the body and look at it from somewhere,

The sophroliminal level which we "enter" during the exercise, is an exciting one, we unite with sensations and melt into that experience. This level stimulates our imagination. Here we can recover our taste for something, craving for something, find our motivation; we reconnect with ourselves and we can even revive the love for painting, music, or other long forgotten passions. We rediscover ourselves. Accessing and remaining at this level is rebalancing, restructuring, and tranquilizing. Sometimes, after an exercise, we feel like we have had a reinvigorating nap.

The first time I did a sophrology exercise I wrote the following pheno-description:

Even after the exercise, I felt the need to breathe deeply in order to calm down my internal "fire".

Who knows what the alien found in my energetic body.

I easily found happy moments."

Dorna Revie, the sophrology teacher, explained to me it's a good idea to write all these things and continue to practice. "Won't it be great when your soul is out of its cage? By regular practice this should happen all by itself."

Directing attention to the inside of one's body connects us with ourselves on a deeper level, and we become aware of phenomena we did not know were there but which were pulsating subliminally in our bodies.

Rainbow exercise

PRE-SOPHRONIC INFORMATION.

This exercise is usually one of the first to be done in a sophrology session because it is pleasant and playful, and often preferred by people. After the basic sophronisation, we will continue, using breath, to release physical and emotional tensions then we will think of all the colors of the rainbow, one by one; we can easily notice the effects of the colors on the body, and this helps us become acquainted with an awareness of the sensations in the body.

You will become aware of the whole body, as if for the first time, exploring it with curiosity from top to bottom. I will name each part of the body, and I just want you to notice it. Keep an open curious attitude and try to collect as many sensations as possible that you will write about afterward in your journal.

After the integration pause, we will complete the exercise.

BASIC SOPHRONISATION.

Please chose a quiet place, turn off your phone, sit down with your feet on the floor, and make yourself comfortable.

Close your eyes so you can concentrate better on what is happening inside. If the eyes are open you can be more easily distracted, but if you prefer to stay with your eyes open, it is fine too.

Become aware of your body as if it is for the first time...

become aware of the sounds outside the room... the sounds inside the room...

and the sounds of your own body, breathing... heart beat...

welcome these sounds as being part of life, without trying to work out what they are...

now focus on your head, become aware of all the sensations...

become aware of your forehead, eyes, muscles around your eyes...

everything that happens in and around the ears...

nose, the air going in and the air going out...

jaw and mouth...

and back of the head...

move your attention down to the neck and throat...

observing everything that happens in the shoulders, the outside part of the arms, elbow, wrist, hand and fingers, all the sensations that arise...

then become aware of your chest, everything inside, the upper part of the back and the inside part of the arms, hands, palm and fingers, noticing with curiosity all the physical sensations...

now draw your attention to the middle part of the body between the chest and waist...

the middle part of the back...

and the internal organs...

become aware of your hips, noticing all the sensations inside and outside this area...

thighs... go down to the legs, knees, lower legs, ankles, feet, toes...

become aware of the whole of the body as if it is for the first time...

notice the weight of the body...

the temperature...

the shape and size of the body...

all the feelings and sensations are welcome...

INTRA-SOPHRONIC ACTIVATION.

Breathe out fully emptying the stomach and lungs...

breathe in deeply, hold your breath, bring your hands above the head and tense the whole body...

and release....

and keep releasing all the tensions by breathing them out, all the tensions, physical, emotional tensions from the body, everything you don't want anymore...

become aware of the color red...

everything becomes red as if you are looking through a red filter and notice all the physical sensations that appear...

then the color orange, bright juicy orange...

and notice the impact of this color on your body... how you feel... perhaps one area of the body has more intense sensations...

become aware of the color yellow, like the yellow of the sun, noticing if these colors have the same effects on your body or are perhaps different...

everything becomes now green inside and outside... like the green of nature... notice the phenomena arising...

concentrate your attention on the color blue like the sky...

and become aware of the impact this color has on your body...

then indigo, like the sky at night...

noticing the sensations... and where... what does this color want to tell you... observe how you feel...

become aware of the color violet, like a lavender field, and the interaction of this color with your body...

...now leave the colors...

THE INTEGRATION PAUSE.

Become aware of the breathing, your body is breathing and you don't have to do anything for that...

notice what happens now in your body...

stay for a few moments melting into the present moment...

you are now, here...

DE-SOPHRONISATION.

Move your body starting with the toes...
let your body move as it wants and feels,
stretch, notice physical sensations...
and only when you are ready, open your eyes and
write in your journal what you have experienced and
observed during the exercise.

Write your FENO-DESCRIPTIONS in the journal.

"A very pleasant exercise,
I felt full of energy and happiness.
I felt best at the green color.
I felt how a `warmth` was going to each part of the
body I was told to focus on."

"I feel very relaxed.
At the red color I felt energy, at the green sleep,
at violet as if I woke up. I felt a yellow light
in my whole body, as if I'm healing."
"Colors: red - excitement, fright, green - sensation of
relaxation (I'm stretching myself),
orange - I swam in orange, wellbeing, freedom,
total comfort.
Parts of the body: the heart, vessels,

vascularisation, beating, motion,
pulse in the cheeks. I saw my body as if
I were lying on my back and looking up,
everything seems huge."

Mood lifting exercise

PRE-SOPHRONIC INFORMATION.

*This exercise changes our mood through the
activation of positive memories and trains our brain to focus
more and more on the positive aspects of life. We notice
what our body does when we feel good, where and how we
feel these positive emotions in the body, underlying at the
same time the importance of these thoughts and their
effects on our body. By repeating the exercise and gathering
as many pleasant memories and events as possible, we feel
happier.*

*After the basic sophronisation we will continue,
using breath, to release all the tensions and then we will
recall memories or events that made us feel good and we
will relive these memories as if they are happening now,
observing with curiosity and wonder all the physical
sensations. We will activate all our senses and we'll try to
collect as many of them as you can, so we can write them
in the journal.*

*After the integration pause we will complete the
exercise.*

BASIC SOPHRONISATION.

Please chose a quiet place, turn off your phone, sit down, feet on the floor, and make yourself comfortable.

Close your eyes so you can concentrate better on what is happening inside. If the eyes are open you can be more easily distracted, but if you prefer to stay with your eyes open, this is fine too.

Become aware of your body as if you do this for the first time...

become aware of sounds outside the room... the sounds inside the room...

and the sounds of your own body, breathing... heart beat...

welcome these sounds as being part of life, without trying to work out what they are...

now focus on your head, become aware of all the sensations...

especially on your forehead, eyes and muscles around your eyes...

everything that happens in and around the ears...

nose, the air going in and the air going out...

jaw and mouth...

and back of the head...

move your attention down to the neck and throat...
observing everything that happens in the
shoulders, the outside part of the arms, elbow, wrist, hand
and fingers, all the sensations that arise...

then become aware of your chest, everything that's
happening inside, the upper part of the back and the
inside part of the arms, hands, palm and fingers, noticing
with curiosity all the physical sensations...

now focus your attention on the middle part of the
body between the chest and waist...
the middle part of the back...
and the internal organs...

become aware of your hips, noticing all the
sensations inside and outside this area...
thighs... go down to the legs, knees, lower legs,
ankles, feet, toes...

become now aware of the whole of the body as if it
is for the first time...
notice the weight of the body...
the temperature...
the shape and size of the body...
all the feelings and sensations are welcome...

INTRA-SOPHRONIC ACTIVATION.

Breath out fully emptying the lungs...

breath in deeply, hold your breath, bring your hands above the head and tense the whole body...

and release....

and keep releasing all the tensions by breathing them out, physical tensions, emotional tensions from the body, everything you don't want anymore...

observe how you breathe... and the physical sensations that are there...

become aware of the whole body from the top of the head to the top of the toes... all the sensations are welcome...

stay for a few moments deep in this very moment...

now think of something that makes you happy, something that you like to do, a moment that gave you pleasure or joy, when you really felt good and relive it as if it were happening now...

notice what happens in your body...

what sensations arise when you activate this good memory...

become aware of the senses, listen to the sounds...

notice the colors...

smell...

touch...

taste...

relive the positive sensations given by that moment... as if it were happening now...

choose another happy moment that occurred recently and relive it now, noticing with curiosity what your body does when you think of something that makes you happy...

to access even more pleasant memories, search in your memory another happy event which brings you a total state of joy and wellbeing... activate all your senses and notice what your body does in these moments...

THE INTEGRATION PAUSE.

Stay for a while in this pose, savoring the sensations given by the depth of your being...

you are here, now...

DE-SOPHRONISATION.

Move your body starting with the toes...
let your body move as it wants and feels...
stretch, notice the physical sensations...
and only when you are ready open your eyes and write in your journal what you have experienced and observed during the exercise.

Write your FENO-DESCRIPTIONS in the journal.

"I relaxed when I started to become aware of my body, but not right from the start. Then, it was

as though my mind calmed down.

I thought of someone I love and I miss,

I relived moments that fill me with love. I feel full of love."

"During this journey the following things happened: it was a strange kind of relaxation.

It was a process and my body

begun to relax at different kind of levels.

In the first place, my body begun to relax when at the same time some colorful

feathers appeared as a picture,

as though it was an Indian ceremony.

I also become aware of another level of relaxation, where I felt shivers in my body.

I relaxed even more and at some point I think I lost contact

with the place, feeling only a smooth

`emptiness` in my body. Shivers came again, and happy

memories came back as a picture – memories I would love to live again."

"Quiet, relaxed, warmth.

I haven't felt so calm for a long time."

Stimulating creativity – interconnecting the brain hemispheres

As Anca Munteanu described, "Besides this variety of methods, from the perspective of creativity it is important that relaxation (being in a twilight state between wakefulness and sleep) increases access to the fountains of the unconscious, using the valuable functions of the right cerebral hemisphere more wisely." Sophrology offers some simple exercises to interconnect both brain hemispheres, which if practiced regularly, helps us concentrate better, be more lucid, and improves our memory, imagination and creativity. They have to be practiced regularly (daily).

Sit comfortably and deeply relax your muscles...
close your eyes...
breathe deeply, slowly, take a few abdominal breaths...

(You can perform for a deeper relaxation, all the basic sofronization process.)

Imagine a black horse with your left eye and a white horse with your right eye at the same time, or vice versa. Do this or a few seconds then unify the images in the center to view one single gray horse. You can change this exercise by imagining any object, geometric shape or color.

Another version of the exercise is to "listen" simultaneously with the right ear a favorite melody and with the left ear another melody, from a different kind of music. Then reunite them.

Write your FENO-DESCRIPTIONS in the journal.

"While viewing the horses separately, I felt a
`concentration` in the brain to keep them like that,
    and when I merged the image
    into one gray horse, the concentration was also
`united`. Interesting!
    My attention has increased."

Three breathing exercises

So as we can enjoy the benefits of deep breathing, we have to exercise it, not only to read and think "it sounds nice, but I'll do them later" or "tomorrow" out of convenience. It is recommended to exercises on an empty stomach or one or two hours after a meal. Below are three different types of breathing exercises. Practice them and see what your body says, what it likes, when it feels better and pay attention to the energy flow of the body. Then write the pheno-descriptions in your journal.

1. This type of breathing is very efficient in oxygenating and calming the whole body and some people feel energized after doing it:
– Inhale slowly and deeply through your nose, until the stomach becomes like a balloon;
– Move the air from the stomach into the lungs, so the stomach empties, then move the air to the shoulders and only now exhale through your mouth;
– Repeat this breathing several times, slowly, without forcing anything;
– Pay attention to the breathing and to everything happening in the body.

2. This breathing exercise increases your concentration, oxygenates the brain, soothes and revitalizes the mind:
– Cover your right nostril with your thumb and inhale only through the left one;
– Hold the breath for one second, covering the left nostril, and exhale through the right one and then inhale through the right one;
– Hold it for a second, cover the right nostril and exhale through the left nostril, then inhale through the left one;
– Do 20 breaths (10 for each nostril).

So, after you have exhaled through one nostril, inhale with the same one before you switch.

3. This exercise is done with the hands folded under the arms, as if you embrace yourself. Breath in, just into the lungs, 36 times without hurrying, noticing what happens in the body. Around the 15th breath, your breathing becomes deeper, gentler and more pleasant. This breathing is effective for people who want to improve their sleeping.

The perfect stress-less day

Imagine what a full working day would look like if you follow the ideas presented in this book, knowing that we can easily transform a working day into a peaceful and calm experience. How would it feel? How would it be?

Starting the day

The alarm wakes you up. Breathe deeply. Focus all your attention on your body. Stretch like a cat and stand up. Breakfast? Of course. But even if you only drink a coffee or a tea, transform it into a moment that matters. Sit down and whatever you are having, taste it, savor it and enjoy it! (This is not going to take you longer!). Pay attention as well to the other activities you do, like showering and getting dressed. Do nothing on the run today.

Going to the job

Even if you go by public transport or by car, you can use this time to relax. You find it hard to believe? Waiting for the tram or the green light? Use any waiting time during the day to relax. Even when you are waiting for your computer to switch on, or for anything else. Breath, bring your shoulders down, check if there are tensions in your body and if there are, release them. Even if you don't want or you can't practice any breathing techniques, just try to breathe a bit more slowly and deeply, easily, without forcing anything.

At work

Take a break before you are tired. You will restore your energy much more quickly, be effective and feel alert much longer. Here are a few ideas:

Sit down, close your eyes, unclench your jaws, relax your shoulders, concentrate on the contact of your feet with the floor and breathe out, loudly;
Several times during the day, check with yourself "Am I breathing?" Yes, but how? Where? How

does it feel? Do you like it or would you like to change anything? The secret lies in taking very short breaks several times during the day, 30 seconds can be enough, so you shouldn't be able to make the excuse that you don't have time. It can help you maintain you energy levels in the long term;

In a meeting or when you talk on the phone you can breathe slowly and be aware of it. If you smile while you are on the phone, it will help the conversation to flow more easily and you will also feel better. The caller will know you are smiling. Try this.

Back at home

If your mind is still at work, here is another simple exercise for you. Sit down, close your eyes and visualize yourself leaving work and closing the door firmly behind you. Then visualize yourself in front of your front door; you can feel how you are dressed, how you are standing. Go in the way you usually go in, inserting the key and turning the handle. You go in and stop on the door step and look at what you see inside – the corridor, the room. Go inside and choose a place in the house which you particularly like and settle down. Then, let the images go and listen to how you are feeling. Breathe out, rub your hands and open your eyes. Are you ready for the end of the day?

Use the time when you are cooking dinner, eating or anything else to be fully focused on that and only that, doing one thing at a time.

Going to bed

Allow at least 30 minutes to unwind, without television or any screen or any work-related activity before going to bed. Do something you enjoy, something calm that will gently lead you towards a better night's sleep.

Enjoy this day and if you like it, repeat it!

In conclusion

My journey with sophrology was a shift of the awareness from a very analytic mind into a more balanced and stable state, a smooth passing from thinking into the body. I could say that before sophrology, I was disconnected from my feelings because I was living almost entirely in my head, and I was keeping my emotions in a closed box in my chest. It took me some time to acknowledge and remain in contact with my feelings. By integrating the practice into daily life, I started realizing and capturing the meaning of being Present, a state that makes me feel alive inside, no matter what actions I take.

I will use some analogies to explain Presence in my way. Sometimes it is like a star that lights up the moment I turn my attention to my body. Remaining with the attention in the body, with the light ON, makes me feel vibrant and radiant and I can perceive my energy increasing. The more Present I am, the more vivid I am, which means there are different intensities of the Presence or awareness. We can compare the force of Presence with a light dimmer switch - if you turn it on to the maximum, the room is full of light, and if you turn it on just a little bit, the room is less lighted.

Sometimes I use for the same purpose the analogy of a Christmas tree full of lights. When the lights are ON, the tree is shining beautifully. When my attention is ON, that is, in the body, I shine from inside, and I am happy with no apparent reason. This one is the state I'm aiming for all the time.

In moments of too much mental and emotional turbulences, agitation, or suffering, knowing that the stories created by my mind will not do any good, I decided to move. I moved my attention from my mind into my body, just noticing my emotions with openness and curiosity and increasing the light as much as I could, both at the same time. I can tell you for sure that this shift of awareness works wonderfully. When we magnify our state of consciousness and Presence, emotions dissipate, thoughts quiet down, and what remains is a state of joy and calm.

Along the way, the teachings of Eckhart Tolle, which represented obligatory bibliography in studying sophrology, were the most valuable resources that helped me enter more and more into the depths of my being and discovering my light.

Bibliography:

"Incursiuni în Creatologie" (*Insights of Creatology*) – Dr. Prof. Anca Munteanu, Augusta Publishing House, Timişoara, 1999;

"The power of now" – Eckhart Tolle, Curtea Veche Publishing, Bucharest, 2009;

"Bazele psihologiei generale" (*The Fundamentals of General Psychology*) – Prof. univ. dr. Mihai Golu, University Publishing House, Bucharest, 2005;

"Being in balance" – Dr. Wayne Dyer, Spirit and Destiny Publishing House, Bucharest, 2015;

"Psychology" – Bernstein, Roy, Srull, Wickens, Houghton Mifflin Publishing, Second Edition;

"Practicioner Diploma Course" – Dorna Revie, Energy Centre Sàrl, Geneva, 2011;

"La sophrologie ici et maintenant" – Académie Suisse de Sophrologie, 2010;

"Decouvrir la sophrologie" – Pascal Gautier, InterEditions, Paris, 2011;

"Le Nouveau Guide Practique de la Sophrologie" – Dr. Y. Davrou, Paris, Retz.

Resources:

www.sofrologia.com
https://www.youtube.com/watch?v=_T0bhDSOmVI
https://en.wikipedia.org/wiki/Sophrology
www. executivesecretary.com – Florence Parot
www.energycentre.ch

About the author

Lorena Luchian is a psychologist, psychotherapist, and sophrologist, and the author of articles written for women`s magazines and publications of a scientific and medical nature. She has been trained in integrative therapy and sophrology and has attended numerous courses, seminars, and conferences related to mental health. Together with the individual study, all these have enriched her knowledge to use a multidirectional and a holistic approach to her clients. As a psychologist, she runs her psychology praxis by offering one-to-one and online sessions to her clients.

The author wrote this book wishing to share with the readers her knowledge and the application of sophrology, the holistic therapy which studies human consciousness in harmony.

Thank you!

I hope you enjoyed my book.
Your feedback is very
important to me.

Please let me know how you liked
the book at:

sofrologie.ro@gmail.com

www.ingramcontent.com/pod-product-compliance
Lightning Source LLC
Chambersburg PA
CBHW071203130726
47998CB00002B/591